F
S

TOFFEE
RECIPES

compiled by
Carol Wilson

with illustrations by
Birket Foster RWS

SALMON

Index

Acid Drops   15
Angus Toffee   38
Barley Sugar   5
Bonfire Toffee   7
Brechin Tablet   42
Bulls-eyes   40
Butterscotch   8
Caramels   6
Chocolate Caramels   46
Chocolate Nut Fudge   16
Chocolate Rum Truffles   26
Cinder Toffee   22
Claggum   31
Coconut Ice   13
Creamy Vanilla Fudge   39
Edinburgh Rock   23
Everton Toffee   34

Glasgow Toffee   18
Honey Fudge   10
Humbugs   24
Golden Toffee   29
Kendal Mint Cake   35
Lollipops   3
Marshmallows   37
Mealie Candy   27
Nougat   11
Nut Brittle   43
Panocha   19
Peppermint Creams   32
Real Fruit Jellies   21
Scots Tablet   14
Sherbet   30
Toffee Apples   45
Turkish Delight   47

Cover pictures: *front:* 'Children paddling' *back:* 'Cowslip gatherers'
title page: 'The bird's nest'

Printed and Published by J. Salmon Ltd., Sevenoaks, England ©

Lollipops

The name 'lolly-pops' in the eighteenth century simply meant 'sweets'. They gained their characteristic shape and stick at the beginning of the twentieth century.

1 lb 1 oz granulated sugar   **4 oz liquid glucose (sold in chemists)**
7 fluid oz water   **Wooden sticks or skewers**
Food colouring and flavouring to individual choice

Place the sticks or skewers on sheets of non-stick baking paper, spaced well apart. Put the water and sugar into a heavy pan over a low heat and stir until the sugar has dissolved. Skim off the white scum from the surface and stir in the glucose. Partially cover the pan and boil rapidly for a few minutes until a little of the mixture when dropped into cold water forms hard but not brittle threads (284°F/144°C on a sugar thermometer). Add a few drops of colouring and flavouring as desired and return to the heat until a little of the mixture tested in cold water separates into hard, brittle threads (312°F/155°C). Remove from the heat and stand for a minute or two before carefully pouring or spooning over the sticks to make lollipop shapes. When completely cold remove from the non-stick paper and wrap individually in clingfilm.

Barley Sugar

A clear, hard sweet which was popular in the eighteenth century and was originally made by boiling sugar in water in which barley had been boiled.

1 lb granulated or caster sugar   **¼ teaspoon cream of tartar**
¼ pint water   **1 tablespoon golden syrup**
Juice of 1 small lemon

Place the sugar and water in a heavy pan and heat gently until the sugar has dissolved. Remove from the heat and stir in the cream of tartar and the golden syrup. Boil until a little of the mixture forms a hard ball when dropped into cold water (247°F/119°C on a sugar thermometer), then reduce the heat and boil gently until a little of the mixture dropped into cold water forms a 'hard crack' (310°F/154°C). Remove from the heat and place the base of the pan in cold water for 5 seconds to cool the mixture. Carefully stir in the lemon juice, then pour into a greased shallow tin. When firm enough to handle cut in strips, twist and place on a cold, oiled surface to harden. Wrap in greaseproof paper and store in an airtight tin.

Caramels

The word caramel appeared in England in 1725 and comes from the Spanish caramelo *which derived from the Latin* calamus *which means cane or reed and referred to sugar cane.*

8 oz granulated or caster sugar	**4 tablespoons water**
2 oz glucose (sold in chemists)	**4 tablespoons milk**
1 tablespoon golden syrup	**½ teaspoon vanilla essence**

Put all the ingredients, except the essence, into a large, heavy pan and heat gently until the sugar has dissolved. Cook gently, stirring from time to time, until a little of the mixture dropped into cold water forms a hard ball between finger and thumb (255°F/124°C on a sugar thermometer). Add the essence, stir and pour into a buttered, shallow tin. Mark into pieces when half set and cut when cold. Wrap in greaseproof paper and store in an airtight tin.

Bonfire Toffee

This is known as 'Plot Toffee' in some parts of Yorkshire, where it is traditionally enjoyed on Bonfire Night, November 5th.

8 oz Demerara sugar   8 oz black treacle
4 oz butter

Melt the butter in a heavy pan and add the treacle and sugar. Heat gently until the sugar has dissolved, then simmer gently for 30 minutes. Test by dropping a little of the mixture in cold water – it should separate into hard but not brittle threads (280°F/140°C on a sugar thermometer). Pour into a buttered, shallow tin and mark into squares when almost set. Break into pieces when cold and wrap in greaseproof paper. Store in an airtight tin.

Butterscotch

This buttery confection is thought to have first been made in the nineteenth century in Scotland – hence the name.

1 lb demerara sugar	**½ pint milk**
4 oz butter	**½ teaspoon vanilla essence**

Place the sugar, butter and milk in a heavy pan and heat gently until the sugar has dissolved. Bring to the boil and boil until a little of the mixture tested in cold water separates into hard, but not brittle threads (280°F/140°C on a sugar thermometer). Remove from the heat, stir in the essence and pour into a buttered, shallow tin. Mark into pieces when the toffee has cooled and break when cold.

'The way down the cliff'

Honey Fudge

The distinctive taste of honey adds a special flavour to this fudge. The taste can be subtly altered by using different types of honeys, for instance: clover honey *is very sweet with a delicate grassy scent;* orange blossom honey *has a flavour of orange peel and almonds while* acacia honey *is the sweetest of all honeys with a heavily scented floral taste.*

2 oz butter   **2 tablespoons honey**
4 tablespoons water   **1 lb granulated sugar**
8 tablespoons condensed milk

Place all the ingredients into a heavy pan and stir over a low heat until the sugar has dissolved. Bring to the boil and boil for about 10 minutes until a little of the mixture dropped into cold water forms a soft ball when rolled between finger and thumb (238°F/114°C on a sugar thermometer). Leave to cool until just warm. Beat well until the mixture becomes thick and creamy and pour at once into a buttered, flat tin. Cut into squares when set.

Nougat

The name of this chewy confection comes from the Latin nux *which means nut and originally walnuts would have been used in the recipe. Nougat is now usually made with almonds instead.*

8 oz blanched almonds, roughly chopped
4 oz honey

4 oz icing sugar
2 egg whites
Rice paper

Put the honey, sugar and egg whites into a heavy pan, stir once to combine and heat gently until the mixture is thick and white and a little of the mixture dropped into cold water forms a hard ball between finger and thumb (247°F/119°C on a sugar thermometer); do not stir during heating. Add the almonds and turn out the mixture on to a surface dusted liberally with icing sugar. Shape into a ball and then press the mixture into a shallow tin lined with rice paper. Cover with more rice paper, then a sheet of non-stick paper. Press down with a similar tin on top containing heavy weights. Leave in a cool place to set, then cut into bars. Wrap in greaseproof paper and store in an airtight tin for up to 2 weeks.

Coconut Ice

*In Victorian times the coconut shy was a popular feature at fairgrounds. The advent
of desiccated coconut, the dried shredded flesh of the nut, led to
its widespread use in cookery.*

1 lb granulated sugar   **5 oz desiccated coconut**
¼ pint milk   **Pink food colouring**

Place the sugar and milk in a heavy pan over a low heat until the sugar has
dissolved. Bring to the boil and cook gently until a little of the mixture dropped
into cold water forms a soft ball between finger and thumb (238°F/114°C on a
sugar thermometer). Remove from the heat and stir in the coconut. Pour half the
mixture quickly into a buttered, shallow tin. Add a few drops of colouring to the
other half, stir and pour quickly over the first half in the tin. Mark into bars and cut
when cold.

Scots Tablet

Tablet has always been a Scottish favourite and is still a best seller at church fetes and bring-and-buy sales.

2 lb granulated sugar	**¼ pint milk**
4 oz butter	**Large tin condensed milk**
¼ pint water	**1 teaspoon vanilla essence**

Put the sugar, butter, water and milk into a large, heavy pan over a low heat and stir until the sugar has completely dissolved. Bring to the boil and boil for 10 minutes without stirring. Stir in the condensed milk and boil for a further 10 minutes. Remove from the heat and add the essence. Beat the mixture for 1 minute, then pour into a buttered, shallow tin and mark into squares. Cut when cold.

Acid Drops

These tart-tasting sweets were first made in the nineteenth century and were called 'acidulated drops'. Their present name came about at the beginning of the twentieth century. In the U.S.A. they are known as sourballs.

1 lb granulated sugar	**¼ teaspoon lemon juice**
¼ pint water	**1 teaspoon tartaric acid**
½ teaspoon cream of tartar	**Icing sugar**

Put the sugar and water into a heavy pan and add the cream of tartar. Heat gently until the sugar has dissolved then boil until the mixture has a yellow tinge. Stir in the lemon juice. Pour on to a cold work surface and work in the tartaric acid with a knife. When the mixture is cool enough to handle, cut into sticks then into small pieces. Form these into small, flat rounds and dust with icing sugar.

Chocolate Nut Fudge

A sweet treat that is ideal for children to make as it is a very simple recipe and needs no cooking.

8 oz plain chocolate   **8 tablespoons evaporated milk**
4 oz butter   **1 lb icing sugar**
4 oz chopped nuts

Melt the chocolate and butter in a bowl over a pan of hot, not boiling, water. Add the evaporated milk and mix well. Sift the icing sugar into the mixture, add the nuts and work it well until the mixture is stiff. Put the mixture into a greased, shallow tin and cut into squares when set.

'The king of the castle'

Glasgow Toffee

In the eighteenth century Glaswegians were fond of making sweets with sugar imported from the West Indies. The women who made and sold this toffee on the city's streets were known as 'Sweetie Wives'.

4 oz butter	**2 oz plain chocolate, grated**
4 oz soft brown sugar	**4 oz golden syrup**
4 oz caster sugar	**¼ pint milk**

¼ teaspoon vanilla essence

Melt the butter in a heavy saucepan. Add the rest of the ingredients, except the essence and bring to the boil. Boil for about 15 minutes, stirring, until a little of the mixture tested in cold water forms hard but not brittle threads (280°F/140°C on a sugar thermometer). Add the essence and pour into a buttered, shallow tin. Mark into squares when cool and break into pieces when cold.

Panocha

An old fashioned sweet that is halfway between fudge and toffee and usually contains nuts.

1 lb soft brown sugar   2 tablespoons butter
5 fluid oz milk   A few drops vanilla essence
1 tablespoon golden syrup   4 oz chopped walnuts

Place the sugar, milk, syrup and butter into a large, heavy pan and bring to the boil, stirring all the time. Boil gently until a little of the mixture dropped into cold water forms a soft ball when rolled between finger and thumb (237°F/114°C on a sugar thermometer). Remove from the heat and leave to stand, without stirring, until lukewarm. Stir in the essence and the walnuts and beat until thick and creamy. Pour into a buttered, shallow tin and mark into squares while warm. Cut when cold.

Cinder Toffee

Adding bicarbonate of soda to the mixture aerates it, producing bubbles in the toffee and altering the texture. When broken into pieces, the toffee looks just like golden coloured cinders.

8 oz granulated or caster sugar	**¼ teaspoon cream of tartar**
	2½ fluid oz water
1 tablespoon golden syrup	**¼ teaspoon bicarbonate of soda**
1 teaspoon warm water	

Put the sugar, syrup, cream of tartar and water into a heavy pan and heat gently until the sugar has dissolved. Boil without stirring until a little of the mixture forms hard, brittle threads when tested in cold water (310°F/154°C on a sugar thermometer). Dissolve the bicarbonate of soda in the teaspoon of warm water and pour it into the toffee, which will froth up. Stir well and pour into a shallow, greased tin. Break into pieces when cold. Wrap in greaseproof paper and store in an airtight tin.

Edinburgh Rock

In the nineteenth century, a young man named Sandy Ferguson created the recipe in his home. It proved so popular with his friends that he decided to go to Edinburgh to make his sweetmeat on a grander scale. Edinburgh Rock is now world famous.

1 lb granulated or caster sugar   **½ teaspoon cream of tartar**
½ pint water   **Icing sugar**
Colouring and flavouring (see below)

Place the sugar and water in a heavy pan over a low heat until the sugar has completely dissolved. Add the cream of tartar and boil the mixture until a hard ball is formed when a little of the mixture is dropped into cold water. (275°F/120°C on a sugar thermometer.) Remove from the heat and stir in a few drops of the flavouring of your choice. Leave to cool for a few minutes. When cool, pour on to an oiled slab and gently turn the edges into the middle with an oiled knife. Repeat this process until the mixture cools and firms. Dust the hands with icing sugar and pull and work the mixture until it becomes dull and harder. Pull for about 10 minutes into strips and then cut into short lengths. Place on a tray lined with greaseproof paper. Leave in a warm place for 24 hours until the rock softens and becomes powdery. Store in an airtight tin lined with greaseproof paper. *Colouring and flavouring: Pink:* raspberry or strawberry essence. *Yellow:* lemon or pineapple essence. *Green:* peppermint oil or essence.

Humbugs

The word humbug was a popular slang term in the eighteenth century and meant a hoax or practical joke. Its use as the name of a sweet seems to have originated in the nineteenth century in the North of England.

1 lb Demerara sugar	**A few drops peppermint oil or**
¼ pint water	**½-1 teaspoon peppermint essence**
2 oz butter	**A pinch of cream of tartar**

Place all the ingredients in a heavy pan over a low heat until the sugar has dissolved. Bring to the boil and cook until a little of the mixture separates into hard but not brittle threads when dropped into cold water. (280°F/140°C on a sugar thermometer) Remove from the heat and cool for 2 minutes. Pour on to an oiled slab and as soon as it is cool enough to handle, pull into long strips. Divide the mixture in half and pull one half until it is much paler than the other. Twist the 2 halves together and cut into short pieces.

Chocolate Rum Truffles

Traditionally eaten at Christmas, these delectable 'melt-in-the-mouth' morsels first appeared in the Army and Navy Stores catalogue of 1926.

6 oz plain chocolate   **2 tablespoons rum**
4 fluid oz double cream   **Cocoa powder or icing sugar for dusting**

Break the chocolate into small pieces. Heat the cream in a saucepan and bring slowly to the boil. Remove from the heat and add the chocolate, stirring until melted. Add the rum and leave the mixture to cool for 30 minutes. Whisk the mixture until it holds its shape, then chill until firm enough to handle. Dust the hands with icing sugar or cocoa powder and shape the mixture into small balls. Roll in icing sugar or cocoa powder and chill. The truffles can be kept in an airtight tin in a refrigerator for up to 3 days.

Mealie Candy

An old Scottish country recipe for a dark, gingery sweetmeat.

**2 oz medium oatmeal   ½ pint water
1 lb granulated sugar   4 oz black treacle
1 dessertspoon ground ginger**

Spread the oatmeal on a baking tray and toast under the grill for a few minutes until golden brown. Put the sugar and treacle into a heavy pan with the water and stir over a low heat until the sugar has dissolved. Bring to the boil and boil for 10 minutes, stirring. Remove from the heat and stir in the oatmeal and ginger. Beat until thick and pour into a greased, shallow tin. Mark into squares and cut when cold.

Golden Toffee

Early in the nineteenth century this sweet was known variously as 'taffy'
or 'tuffy' and was nicknamed 'stickjaw'.

1 lb granulated or caster sugar   **2 teaspoons white wine vinegar**
2 oz butter   **8 oz golden syrup**
1 tablespoon water

Place all the ingredients in a heavy pan and heat gently until the sugar has dissolved. Boil rapidly until a little of the mixture dropped into cold water forms brittle threads (310°F/154°C on a sugar thermometer). Pour into a buttered, shallow tin and mark into squares when almost set. Break into pieces when cold and wrap in greaseproof paper.

Sherbet

The original sherbet was an Arabic drink made from water, sugar and fruit juice. In the nineteenth century a fizzy powder was created with which to make a drink which was meant to resemble the Oriental sherbet. A favourite childhood treat was to dip liquorice sticks and lollipops into a bag of sherbet.

2 lb caster sugar
½ oz citric acid

A few drops of lemon, raspberry or strawberry essence

Put the sugar into a food processor or blender and blend into fine crystals, but not to a powder. Transfer to a bowl, stir in the citric acid and essence and mix very well. Leave to dry and put into a screw-top jar to store. Add 2 heaped teaspoons to a glass of cold water to make a refreshing drink.

Claggum

*This was sometimes known as 'teasing candy' and was very popular
in Scotland at Hogmanay.*

2 teacups black treacle   1 teacup cold water

Put the treacle and water into a heavy pan and warm gently over a low heat. Then boil quickly until a little of the mixture, dropped into cold water forms a soft ball between finger and thumb (238°F/114°C on a sugar thermometer). Pour into a greased, shallow tin. When cool enough to handle, pull out the toffee with hands lightly dusted with flour or icing sugar until it becomes pale and creamy in colour and twist into long sticks.

Peppermint Creams

Sweets were first flavoured with peppermint at the end of the eighteenth century.

1 lb icing sugar   4 tablespoons condensed milk
A few drops of oil of peppermint

Sift the icing sugar into a mixing bowl and add the condensed milk. Mix well until smooth and creamy. Add the peppermint oil and work the mixture with the hands until the flavouring is evenly distributed. Roll out ¼ inch thick on a board dusted with icing sugar and cut into small rounds (size according to preference). Leave in a cool place to set.

Everton Toffee

This is believed to have first been made in the Liverpool district of Everton in 1759 by a Molly Bushell. Her delicious toffee became famous and although the recipe is no longer a secret, is still popular today.

1 lb Demerara sugar   8 oz unsalted butter
1 teacup water   4 tablespoons golden syrup
A few drops of lemon essence

Place the sugar and water in a heavy pan over a low heat until the sugar has dissolved. Add the butter and golden syrup and stir over a medium heat until a little of the mixture dropped into cold water forms hard but not brittle threads (280°F/140°C on a sugar thermometer). Remove from the heat and stir in the lemon essence. Pour into a buttered, shallow tin and mark into squares while still warm. Break into pieces when cold.

Kendal Mint Cake

Made in the town of Kendal in Cumbria for about a hundred years, this energy-giving sweetmeat is popular with walkers and climbers.

1 lb sugar (white or brown)   ¼ pint milk
½–1 teaspoon peppermint essence or
few drops peppermint oil

Dissolve the sugar in the milk in a heavy pan over a low heat. Bring to the boil, stirring constantly and cook until a little of the mixture dropped into cold water forms a soft ball between finger and thumb. (237°F/114°C on a sugar thermometer). Remove from the heat, beat the mixture for 2 minutes then return to the heat and boil again until a little of the mixture when tested forms a firm ball (247°F/119°C). Remove from the heat, add the flavouring and stir until thick. Pour into an oiled, shallow tin and mark into bars. Cut when cold.

Marshmallows

Originating in the nineteenth century, when they were made from an extract of the marsh mallow plant, these soft textured sweets are nowadays made from gelatine and sugar.

6 tablespoons water	1 teaspoon vanilla essence
2 tablespoons gelatine	2 egg whites
1 lb granulated sugar	A pinch of salt
½ pint water	2 oz icing sugar
1 teaspoon golden syrup	1 oz cornflour

Put the 6 tablespoons water into a bowl, sprinkle in the gelatine and leave to soak. Put the sugar and ½ pint of water into a heavy pan and stir over a low heat until the sugar has dissolved. Stir in the golden syrup. Boil until a little of the mixture when dropped into cold water forms a soft ball between finger and thumb (240°F/116°C on a sugar thermometer). Remove from heat and let bubbles subside. Stir in the soaked gelatine until dissolved, then pour into a bowl and leave to cool until just warm. Beat with an electric mixer or a rotary beater until very thick and light and whisk in the essence. Beat the egg whites with the salt until stiff peaks form and gently fold into the mixture using a metal spoon. Pour into a well oiled, shallow tin and leave overnight to set. Combine the icing sugar and cornflour on a clean flat surface. Turn out the marshmallow on to the mixture, cut into cubes with a sharp knife and roll in the sugar mixture until completely coated. Store in an airtight tin.

Angus Toffee

*A Scottish speciality, from the Angus region. This toffee is unusual because
it contains ground almonds.*

1½ lb granulated sugar	**4 fluid oz milk**
1 oz butter	**2 oz ground almonds**

Put all the ingredients into a thick saucepan. Stir well and bring to the boil over a
low heat. Boil for 7 minutes, stirring constantly. Remove from the heat and stir
until the mixture is thick. Pour into a buttered tin and mark into pieces when cool.
Cut in to pieces when cold.

Creamy Vanilla Fudge

The name of this popular sweet is something of a mystery. It first appeared at the end of the nineteenth century, when it was described as a type of 'bonbon'.

1 lb granulated sugar   **¼ pint evaporated milk**
2 oz butter   **¼ pint fresh milk**
A few drops of vanilla essence

Put all the ingredients, except the essence, into a large, heavy pan and heat gently until the sugar has dissolved. Bring to the boil and boil steadily, stirring from time to time, until a little of the mixture dropped into cold water forms a soft ball when rolled between finger and thumb (240°F/115°C on a sugar thermometer). Remove from the heat and place the pan on a cool surface. Stir in a few drops of the essence and beat the mixture until it becomes thick and creamy and starts to 'grain'. At this stage the mixture is thick but still pourable so immediately pour into a buttered, shallow tin and leave to become cold. Cut into squares when set.

Bulls-eyes

These large round sweets were a great favourite in the nineteenth century and are mentioned in the 1857 classic novel Tom Brown's Schooldays.

2 lb granulated sugar	**Yellow food colouring**
¼ teaspoon cream of tartar	**¼ teaspoon lemon essence**
1 teacup cold water	**¼ teaspoon tartaric acid**

Place the sugar, water and cream of tartar in a large, heavy pan over a low heat until the sugar has dissolved. Bring to the boil and boil until a little of the mixture dropped into iced water separates into hard, brittle threads (310°F/154°C on a sugar thermometer). Pour half the mixture on to a cold surface and when cool enough to handle, pull until creamy white in colour. Add the colouring, essence and tartaric acid to the remaining mixture in the pan, pour quickly on to a cold surface and pull the mixture as before. Cut the white part into strips and place on top of the yellow part, leaving 1 inch between each strip. Fold in two with the white stripes outside and cut into pieces. Shape into balls. Wrap in greaseproof paper to store.

Brechin Tablet

A colourful variation of the traditional Scottish favourite which comes from the town of Brechin between Dundee and Aberdeen.

1 lb caster sugar	4 oz chopped walnuts
½ pint single cream	1 oz glacé cherries, chopped
1 tablespoon golden syrup	1 oz angelica, chopped

1 teaspoon vanilla essence

Place the sugar and cream in a heavy pan over a low heat until the sugar has dissolved. Add the golden syrup and stir over a medium heat until boiling. Add the walnuts, cherries and angelica and boil rapidly for 10 minutes. Remove from the heat and stir in the essence. Leave to cool for a few minutes then beat the mixture until it becomes thick and grainy. Pour quickly into a buttered, shallow tin and mark into pieces. Cut when cold and wrap in greaseproof paper to store.

Nut Brittle

The name of this sweet perfectly describes its hard, crunchy texture.

14 oz granulated sugar   **¼ pint water**
6 oz soft brown sugar   **2 oz butter**
6 oz golden syrup   **¼ teaspoon bicarbonate of soda**
12 oz chopped nuts

Place the sugars, syrup and water in a large, heavy pan over a low heat until the sugar has completely dissolved. Add the butter and bring to the boil. Boil gently until a little of the mixture dropped into cold water separates into hard brittle threads (310°F/154°C on a sugar thermometer). Stir in the bicarbonate of soda and the nuts. Pour immediately into a buttered, shallow tin and mark into pieces when almost set. Break when cold.

Toffee Apples

A fairground treat since the Middle Ages, when the apples would have been coated with a mixture of boiling honey and beeswax.

1 lb granulated sugar
2 oz butter
2 teaspoons white wine vinegar
1 tablespoon golden syrup
¼ pint water
6–8 eating apples
Wooden sticks

Place all the ingredients (except the apples and the sticks!) in a heavy pan and heat gently until the sugar has dissolved. Boil rapidly for 5 minutes until a little of the mixture dropped into cold water forms hard but not brittle threads (280°F/140°C on a sugar thermometer). Wipe each apple and push a stick into the core. Dip into the toffee mixture. Swirl around to remove any excess then place on a buttered tin or non-stick baking paper to set. Eat on the day they are made.

'Burying the favourite'

Chocolate Caramels

The addition of chocolate makes these chewy caramels even more of a treat. The first solid eating chocolate was created in 1847 and was quickly incorporated into many popular recipes of the time.

1 oz butter	8 tablespoons golden syrup
¼ pint condensed milk	2 oz cocoa powder
8 oz caster sugar	½ teaspoon vanilla essence

Melt the butter in a large, heavy pan and add the milk, sugar and syrup. Stir over a low heat until the sugar has dissolved, then bring to the boil. Add the cocoa and continue boiling until a little of the mixture dropped into cold water forms a hard ball between finger and thumb (255°F/124°C on a sugar thermometer). Stir in the essence and pour into a buttered shallow tin. Mark into pieces when half set and break when cold.

Turkish Delight

This Turkish sweetmeat is called Rahat Lokoum *(literally 'throat's ease') in its home country and was originally known in English as 'Lumps of Delight'. Its present name was first recorded in 1877.*

½ pint water
1 oz gelatine
1 lb granulated sugar
¼ teaspoon citric acid
1 oz cornflour

1 tablespoon rosewater
A few drops of pink food colouring
1 oz icing sugar

Put the water into a pan and sprinkle in the gelatine. Add the sugar and citric acid and stir over a low heat until the sugar has dissolved. Boil over a medium heat for 20 minutes then add the rosewater and colouring. Leave to cool for 15 minutes then pour into a very well oiled, shallow tin. Leave to set for 24 hours. Combine the icing sugar and cornflour on a clean flat surface, turn out the jelly on to this mixture and cut into cubes with a sharp knife. Roll the cubes in the sugar mixture until completely coated and leave on a wire rack to dry for a few hours. Then put into a container and pack with more icing sugar and cornflour in equal quantities.

METRIC CONVERSIONS

The weights, measures and oven temperatures used in the preceding recipes can be easily converted to their metric equivalents.

Weights

Avoirdupois	Metric
1 oz.	just under 30 grams
4 oz. (¼ lb.)	app. 115 grams
8 oz. (½ lb.)	app. 230 grams
1 lh	454 grams

Liquid Measures

Imperial	Metric
1 tablespoon (liquid only)	20 millilitres
1 fl. oz.	app. 30 millilitres
1 gill (¼ pt.)	app. 145 millilitres
½ pt.	app. 285 millilitres
1 pt.	app. 570 millilitres
1 qt.	app. 1.140 litres

Oven Temperatures

	°Fahrenheit	Gas Mark	°Celsius
Slow	300	2	140
	325	3	158
Moderate	350	4	177
	375	5	190
	400	6	204
Hot	425	7	214
	450	8	232
	500	9	260

Flour as specified in these recipes refers to Plain Flour unless otherwise described.